Guide to Happiness

Boot Camp for the Twenty-First Century

DENIZA D.C.FITU

BALBOA.
PRESS

A DIVISION OF HAY HOUSE

Balboa Press books may be ordered through booksellers or by contacting:

Balboa Press
A Division of Hay House
1663 Liberty Drive
Bloomington, IN 47403
www.balboapress.com
1 (877) 407-4847

Because of the dynamic nature of the Internet, any web addresses or links contained in this book may have changed since publication and may no longer be valid. The views expressed in this work are solely those of the author and do not necessarily reflect the views of the publisher, and the publisher hereby disclaims any responsibility for them.

The author of this book does not dispense medical advice or prescribe the use of any technique as a form of treatment for physical, emotional, or medical problems without the advice of a physician, either directly or indirectly. The intent of the author is only to offer information of a general nature to help you in your quest for emotional and spiritual well-being. In the event you use any of the information in this book for yourself, which is your constitutional right, the author and the publisher assume no responsibility for your actions.

Any people depicted in stock imagery provided by Thinkstock are models, and such images are being used for illustrative purposes only. Certain stock imagery © Thinkstock.

Printed in the United States of America.

ISBN: 978-1-4525-8886-5 (sc)
ISBN: 978-1-4525-8887-2 (e)

Balboa Press rev. date: 07/11/2014

"Spread the word to those who have heard but may have forgotten. This is the day of the assumption" ANON

Dedicated to my sons Andrei and Deniz. Through them I was inspired to complete this hard, but so worthy task! The purity of God I see in them I want to find in myself and others.

Dedicated also to Mr. Don, the father
of my soul, always an infant.

Dear Reader,

You should know from the beginning, The Blessed Mother and Lord Jesus are the parental- and the human models for my belief system. In this system the human heart is one with the Immaculate Conception, the Blessed Mother, with whom the human mind is reborn. Now the child of this heart has a mind which lives in a loving, safe home- the brain, the Father one with the mind, the Son.

"Guide to Happiness" directs our attention to the purity of love in the human heart. In this purity we unify with our Lord, Jesus Christ. This unification eliminates fear, frustration and judgment and the healthy balance is restored.

Because the force and essence of life live in a happy and calm heart, I believe here lays the key of energy for all creative thinking different from the competitive one. When we discover that life's force is the Man's love we can have heaven on earth. Now our own thoughts are based on His justice where His love produces an ordered brain seen in society. This program is for those ready to "die" which means separate from the old beliefs based on fear, sadness, regrets in order to find new beliefs. This new beliefs are based on real spirit of life, love, courage and intelligence. From this principal we proceed to the mission of this core belief. The mission of this core belief is the use of the free will - our greatest gift- to gain the power of good decision. But _good decisions have to be based on real power_: _love_ and _gentleness_. This is my faith and my life's fundamental principal which has unlimited potential to _combat ever-present conflict_, our _constant enemy_. Continuous conflict invites a host of health disorders involving the heart and the nerves which translates into diabetes, cancer and all the rest. I strongly believe we must identify these conflicting circumstances or situations, (social, opposing, competitive, for example) in order to treat them. We learn to deal with conflict as it manifests from childhood into adulthood. As children we understand from the purity of love not from the damaged version of it! When the purity of love between our parents and our parents and us is uneasy, our brain is confused and our life goes the same. This unseen, well-kept unconsciously secret is very clearly seen in our faulty, conflicted decisions.

If we are not willing to change our belief about enlightened self-love our lives are broken, and our children will mirror us, the damaged blue print. This is crucial - we either make it or break it. Because I am one of these children, and a parent as well, I am experienced and prepared to write this guide.

I have been searching for decades for a lifesaver such as "Guide to Happiness". After 40 years of reading, studding and traveling the whole world I was prepared *to do* everything from this program. After 4 years of concentrated effort to write in a second language, I offer it now to you. It is my fond hope it will be your lifesaver.

Clearly, this guide is not for everyone. It speaks to the few who are ready to *change their thinking* in order to improve their lives. Otherwise, pain is inevitable. Ready? Please proceed.

Contents

I

About the Author

Deniza Doina Fitu is a certified Reflexologist - Manzanares Reflexologic Method from the School for Healing Arts & Massage, Michigan, and an accredited instructor of Irwin's Heart & Sole Reflexology Program of the same school respectively. She is the founder of "Heal N.O.W."- nothing ordinary works, and author of "Guide to Happiness" G.T.H., Boot Camp for the 21st Century.

Deniza D's first contact with Reflexology was the year she became a mother, 1985. She was fondling her son's ears, or holding the back of his lobes with her four fingers. With her thumb she was applying pressure. The result was always the same; the baby falls asleep. Later she learned that what she had done was apply a basic technique used in Science of Reflexology. Reflexology teaches that every nerve has a neuro-bio-chemical path to follow. The effect of the reflexologic magnetic stimulation affects brain waves. This brings relaxation to the brain and can be seen in neuro- physiologic images that are body, or mirror-like in nature. Because Deniza D. has been in this field for many years, she understands this therapy's effect on the brain and how this relaxation promotes serenity and health. To serve better her clients, she introduced the concept of emotional guidance through her practice of Reflexology. Emotional guidance is based on an enlightened development of the self-love, an achievement that introduced a level of clarity, by changing behavioral patterns in thinking. This induced happiness to her own life. This self-love means the recognition" that the Divine is the center and the sources of all good". S.O.M, Ernest Holmes

Adding to her accomplishments, Deniza D. earned a Bachelor of Law degree while living in Romania from the prestigious Petre Andrei University of Iasi. Parenthetically Iasi is Balkan's cultural center.

After arriving in Michigan, 2002, she specialized in Science of Reflexology-Manzanares Reflexologic Method under the guidance of Charlotte Irwin, instructor of Dr. Manzanares M.D. This scientist established that Reflexology is a hard science that works in Central Nervous System which includes the reticular formation. This reticular formation shows the map of the infant shaped body, perhaps the center of all emotions. She received much insight into what it means to apply this marvelous healing technique of reflexology. Deniza D. immersed herself in understanding this concept as a naturist medicine, founding herself within the science and behaviors of the central nervous system. As her mind developed dimensionally through her studies and work, Doina's life transitioned as well. She relocated to Arizona and established a new home. Here she was able to create this awesome, well-structured program, "Guide to Happiness" G.T.H., Boot Camp for 21st Century. Her most meaningful accomplishment comes last; she is a proud mother of two sons.

Deniza D. was born and educated in Iasi, Romania's esteemed spiritual center. It has been said Romania is Blessed Mother's garden, where 98% of population has orthodox beliefs. She is proudly one of the majority. Raised in communist setting while spending her childhood in an orthodox culture, reasoning of people around her were deeply and profoundly skewed and confused. In her early years of family life, this confusion was aggravated because of her incurable love, compassion and curiosity about Jesus and Mary. This love was sweetly expressed by the example of her grandmothers both Mary. They took care of her in two lovely villages until she was 7. Later, unfortunately, she went in the city to go to school and live with her parents. The loving perception of love for her from the grandmothers was not matched in the parental home. But the base formed from the village drove her to know and to do things to please people. Unfortunately without the right parental love she failed to love herself. She always believed is surrounded with love but she didn't know she had to practice enlightened self-love and she didn't know how! Of course this means she was poorly prepared for life, especially the family life to come. Without any human been to give her comfort or advice, she lost some hope in future.

Recognizing that she is powerless she delivered her life to Mother Mary. Mother Mary then inspired her with "Guide to Happiness". This venture is exciting and has changed her life, and life of others.

The author is only the guide for this program, but not just any guide; to some extent she will be also the interpreter.

It is time to meet Virginia, who lived a life like mine, a middle aged woman and a single mother. Here is her experience as a patient with "Heal N.O.W.".-nothing ordinary works, and "Guide to Happiness" G.T.H., Boot Camp for 21st Century".

Virginia's recent life

Four years ago, Virginia was physically, financially and emotionally broken. Overwhelmed with stress, she thinks "is everybody wrong except me? Perhaps I need correction and I am not aware of it?" She enrolled in "Quantum Energy Psychology" school and learned that the human soul drives each human being's life. Using these school methods, she saw herself - a young child crying, yearning, for love and protection. In fact, she was isolated — there was neither love nor protection. Interestingly enough, Virginia temporarily benefited from these educational methods. Unfortunately, her school emphasized emotional life, or rather, emotional intelligence as a part of life to the detriment of the mental growth process. For Virginia, this was unacceptable; it was placing "the cart before the horse", the mind has to be first. Learning about my skills—my "gift" - by referrals, Virginia came to me for help. At the outset I took her medical history.

She proceeds: "I am very tired and tense. My body seems worn out and, as you can see, I have been treated recently for several physical disorders."

I stated softly: "Since childhood experiences make or break our adult life, I need to learn about your childhood in some pertinent detail".

Virginia shared her early childhood story: "At age two my parents divorced. My father, the idol of my life, was soon gone and I was emotionally devastated. As for my mother, besides being a perfectionist, she tended to be very moody -cold but at times, paradoxically, this behavior gave way to spells of blazing anger. I felt alone, rootless and fearful. However I retained my craving for the sweetness of parental love and the protection that goes with it. For many years this craving for family love remained. Therefore I strove more than once to create and nurture family life, but failed. Because of my yearning for a family of my own, my body deteriorated, where I experienced a break down to the tune of nine physical disorders."

About Guide to Happiness

I explained to Virginia: The program entitled, "Guide to Happiness" inserted into "Heal N.O.W."-<u>nothing ordinary works</u> may help you. The Guide combines alternative western medicine with prayer and positive affirmations. Patients repeat to themselves, in a relaxed frame of mind, *the healing affirmations, in the present tense-as if the action has already taken place.* The prayer I use often for myself ,I use as a practitioner: "Much gratitude to God, the Blessed Mother's Son Our lwho guides and guards your heart as He does mine." Thank you!

These tools free the way to health, wealth and loving relationships.

Reflexology is a useful tool to achieve a calm mind and heart which is necessary for this healing program.

"Guide to Happiness" provides a path to discovering and treating the causes of your symptoms. The cause is usually stress and this program helps you transform stress in to power and vitality. The procedure I use is named D.I.2R. (detection, identification, and removal replacement). Reflexology is necessary to achieve the first step of DI2R.

D-detection is admitting that the body requires serious attention to physical problems.

I-Identification is related to specific people and events, which have caused much hurt (later the body reflects).

2R- Remove the hurt. Replacement has its room. Related with R-removal we turn now to confrontation which is essential. This means recalling specific people and events in a face to face manner so all the hurt is fully exposed to the light. Now, everyone has their own pain -the offender and the one hurt. Virginia, because you understand their pain you are able to have compassion which leads you to your heart. In your heart is love and forgiveness."

This was the overview of what we are doing here. It usually takes about one year to have a heartfelt perception of the reality of your being.

Today, Virginia wants to know more about "The Guide."

About DI2R

Accordingly, I set forth the components and how they work. D.I.2R. is a great benefit to any adult, whom, as a child, was seriously emotionally hurt by parents or others. Parents or others for whatever reason cause damage to the child with words, action and attitude. This damage produces emotional harm. This harm often translates in following the footsteps of those causing the hurt. The child wants to do better and not repeat the behavioral cycles in place -- but those paradigms remain. This means the creation and/or repetition of bad habits. The behavioral patterns become comfortable - familiar now as time passes. Even traumatic at times, for them, they are *reinforced by those who created the model for emotional trauma in the child's life*. This is now normalized or familiar behavior that and is now the blue print for a disjointed, chaotic life. This will not change until the child, now an adult, has decided to find and ***does find***, a better blue print. This is why "Guide to Happiness" exists.

Detection is a realization that specific things have gone wrong. They can be physical, emotional, financial or all of them.

Identification leads to specific action. For better understanding let's examine the experience of Mr. Rob with D.I.2R.

Mr. Rob's problem, aggressive kidney attack, caused an appointment change with me. His mind visualized the empty parking spot.

Mr. Rob recalls D.I.2R.

Detection-he recognized his panic but decided to stop it. His problem is the image of the empty parking spot. He decides to visualize "the car in the parking spot." And he does. Mr. Rob removes the negative image of the empty spot by replacing the empty with the full. He arrives and the car is indeed in its spot. He was instantly cheered; he had an infusion of self-empowerment.

"Wow!" He said "D.I.R. helps my brain achieve -- not just now, but in the future".

Mr. Rob identified problem, "empty" instead of "full" that created the sense of panic.

In the mind of Mr. Rob, it is not surprising that lack of love causes emptiness and hurt, and these both causes panic. This is a condition that existed as a problem from early life. The damage (emotional scaring) leads to low capacity to cope with life, causing much suffering – even self-esteem issues. This suffering often creates panic (high intensity fear). And fear leads to bad decisions.

Remember: good decisions are the purpose of "Guide to Happiness".

Removal-Replacement

Removal is expelling of unloving images. Replacement is inserting the loving. And we wait for our own wholesome self-loving result. Removal and replacement are done simultaneously. Explanation of this is through recall.

Recall:

Mr. Rob formed in his mind the image of an empty spot. He filled the empty spot with the image of the parked car. He has done 2R Removal-Replacement demonstrating an example of the positive image needed.

Removal comes with the hard work through the cleansing of the "mental house". "Cleansing" means dedication in working to remove spiritual impurities thoroughly and completely within one's moral and emotional nature. Of course to the needs of each case must match the requirements of Detection and Identification.

In this cleansing, my job is to learn something specific or germane within the experiences of the parents or individual(s) involved, when appropriate. These experiences may not have auspiciously deserved, but they happened. It is necessary to identify and understand them in order to help the patient become forgiving and loving. Mental stability and the ability to maintain a stable environment is essential, these enable us to make good decisions. In this cleansing process there is a need for validation. Here lies the merit of Reflexology. This is the core for calming the mind, healing the heart, nurturing the feelings and allowing a healthy environment for the process to proceed.

About Science of Reflexology

In the D.I.2R. process, the Science of Reflexology is the major course of treatment. It works within the central nervous system according to valid science. According to science each human brain has an infant body, perfectly shaped, formed from the fetal position. Reference: Student Reflexology Book, Principals of Reflexology (revised) By Manzanares

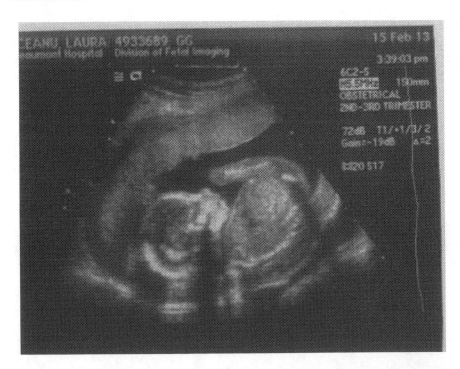

The baby's position in the brain is similar to the fetal position in the mother's womb. (This baby is the gift from God, my granddaughter, now in the fetal position.)

The brain formation of the infant has a corresponding map in each foot.

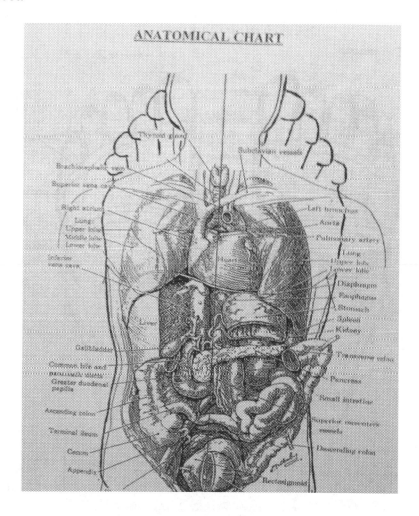

These three maps are connected through nerve endings which are reflex points. The reflex points are stimulated with thumb pressure technique. Applying pressure on the feet the hidden energy activates. *This energy improves circulation* and gives to the brain, body and heart a deep sense of well-being. *The brain*, which *generates electricity*, has now *lower resistance*, for it is *relaxed*. *The brain* gets *more blood;* therefore, *more oxygen*.

In an oxygen rich environment, **the body's chemistry rebalances**, and **toxins are simultaneously released**.

Note: In context of this paper, this is my working definition for Reflexology (for the scientific definition refer to www.manzanaresmethod.com).

Toxicity is most damaging upon the brain. Because of my experience in the field of Reflexology, I believe that *thoughts fed by fear are often the most toxic field for this biochemical organ (the brain). When the oxygen environment of the brain is very low the brain suffers from high level of toxicity. This toxicity affects the infant body shape from the mind that lives now in a polluted environment. When this child is hurt, the brain holds its negative emotion. This becomes the source of negative thoughts and <u>thought is life.</u> Later the unseen hurt is seen in all aspects of the person's life. The physical body, mirror –like, reflects its inner body.* However, Reflexology is a human science. It reduces stress and in some cases gives total relief. But in many cases the cause of stress remains undisturbed. In order to really combat the cause of stress we must go above science.

"What do you mean above science? Please explain," Virginia asked.

I reply: Let's consider the statement of Teresa of Avila "*Why do the hard way? Go to Mary*". Go to Mary means to meditate deeply upon her given prayer, The Holy Rosary. Mother Mary says "*If you love me you will pray my Rosary.*" This meditation opens the "hinges "of the mind, so agreeable to the heart! Obviously we can feel relax since the cause of stress is in the Mother of Hope hands.

"If praying to Mary is above science and The Blessed Mother can take care of my stress, please tell me more!" Virginia exclaims.

About the story of one mother

I said, "Virginia, please permit me to share the story of one loving mother, Nancy Lincoln. Her husband, Tom, was a difficult man. She was kind of a single mother. But Nancy, with her pure love, great courage and belief in her son Abraham, aided him as he elevated to the level of Presidency as the 16th American President. 'Anything I have been in the past, anything I am now, and anything I will ever be, I owe to my angel mother.' Abraham Lincoln.

Virginia, we understand that Nancy gave to her son a powerful foundation for his life. For other children, perhaps like you, The Blessed Mother is waiting in your heart. To connect with her we meditate upon her prayer, The Holy Rosary."

About The Holy Rosary

"*To recite the Rosary is nothing other than to contemplate the face of Christ with Mary.*" Pope John Paul II.

"So Virginia, about The Holy Rosary I tell you as my friend told me, 'The Blessed Mother in person inspired Saint Dominic to create "The Holy Rosary" in thirteen century, 1208. Virginia, as we recall, The Blessed Virgin Mary has prayed to God before Christ on behalf of His children since she was three years old. She was living twelve years in the temple in Jerusalem and prayed daily with humility at the altar. "What is praying with humility?" Virginia asked.

I told her as I was told, "Humility means to know the truth. Compared with God's Spirit, Holy Mother sees her spirit as poor indeed." Now, she knows what it means to be 'poor in Spirit.'

To you, the reader, please note:

There are limitations to human science; however, it does show the way! This means Reflexology and Holy Rosary both stimulate the frontal cortex to produce the neurotransmitter, scrotonin. Science proves that serotonin combats fear and promotes peace. This is such a vital concept!

After some thought, Virginia chose "Guide to Happiness" to be used in her treatment of spiritual, soulful healing and care.

IV

"Guide to Happiness" and its practical applications

To implement D.I.2R. I laid out to Virginia the specifics of "Guide to Happiness" and its practical applications.

a) First part of the guide is detection.

Detection is realization of something chronically wrong, repetition of more than one problem or problems. (The concept includes omission, redundancies, mistakes and errors of sequence, wrong order).They can be physical, emotional, financial or all of the above.

b) The second part of the guide is identification.

For me, identification of a patient's emotional state of mind is essential. I must specifically, learn the severity of emotions or natural behaviors to determine state or frame of mind. This part is very important as I determine course of treatment based upon my findings. It is essential I take the time needed to determine an accurate diagnosis. Therefore, each case varies and takes course of treatment is longer or shorter as needed. Here are 6 powerful (and often complex) steps:

1) Avoid criticism of yourself and others. Make this commitment. Feel married to this commitment and strive never to fail.

2) Accept the negative feelings that cause hurt. They must happen. It is the red signal. Stop and wait for the green.

Now you can proceed to the next step of identification.

3) Face the source of the hurtful experiences which create bad feelings. This is essential.

4) Replace the hurtful faces with those that make your heart feels good. Can be yours. Wish for them what you wish for yourself, always peace, health and happiness.

5) Consciously avoid the negative emotions, use step 4 and elevate your feelings. All this take time but with patience "most people are about as happy as they want to be". (Paraphrase Abraham Lincoln).It is just the free-will. We need to use it. It is free!

6) With free-will you choose your own up-lifting thoughts or wishes, and patiently apply them. I name it 'self-motivation' with "active patience". This is displayed in our everyday roles in life. An example would be parental or guardianship. We assume a protective role in other's lives. In this role, we become parents – but in context of being like a guardian for our own mind. The infant, which is happy and up-lifted, now has a true sense of deliverance within our heart. The heart is the place of origin where all the blessings are given and received. We appreciate and display gratitude for everything good that happens in our life. The notion of well-being, good fortune, dignity, grace. Later, the thought is firmly used as an announcement. In time, passivity dissolves and passion arises. You can see your own results and this leads to wholesome self-love and confidence.

The central nervous system controls and coordinates all organs and structure of the body, including attitude, from passive to action and passion. We need to examine in a greater detail I- identification:

1) Avoid all form of criticism of yourself and others.
   Criticism of yourself and others may be an indicator of low spirituality therefore insecurity. But an insecure person has fear.

What Fear Means And Its Cause

Parents often hurt become fearful. Because of it they are untruthful in life's process. What parents have in their "store" is transmitted to their children. This leads to formation of the wrong self-image. But it is not your image. You are the reflection, mirror-like, of their fearful - obviously untruthful- image of themselves manifested from within life's circumstances. But your own image is the opposite and represents love, trust and joy's image. Fear is so powerful! It stunts the feelings and permits only sluggish growth. It is believed that fear is a response to learned behavior. It is the result of conditioned classical behavior where these fearful images within a person may represent a fear of living life, often unsuccessfully. Therefore, one must identify, recognize and understand that being may be requires "correction". For being fear filled means the need to change thinking – and replace fear with the notion that wholesome, self-love requires rational faith (fear corrodes faith which is love). So then the curious question: How can this person cope with life? Possible answer: Coping is possible only when the person learns wholesome, sound, mentally and behaviorally healthy, love.

About Wholesome Love

One who has wholesome love is humble, grateful, and always prays to fulfill this state of being. Unlike the fearful person, this person naturally loves him or herself and others while naturally accepts the same in return. He takes care of himself and feels fit, powerful and capable of helping others. Without wholesome love, the hurt, unhappy, now fear filled person has a broken spirit with a damaged perception of life and how to treat others. He/she sees everyone as sinful or not good enough - or forms a judgment or skewed opinion - and invites a host of destructive emotions as:

Jealousy: an emotion that happens when a person feels envy, anger, or perpetuates suspicion unnecessarily, which can overtake one's mind, emotion, spirit where the outcome can result in irrational behavior or exchange of irrational, lashing words. It's a low-down and very common emotion. This is a fear where one could feel threatened or a sense of "entitlement" of not having what another person possesses. Be aware! The antidote is blessing what others have and may God give you even better. Pray!

Hatred: is a deep and emotional extreme or (intense) dislike, detest, hostility or animosity toward person, place, thing, or situation. It corrodes the hater first, and threatens everyone it touches. It is so terrible, and so sad. To diminish the hate bless that person and pray: "Lord, please take care of him as you take care of God!" It's impressive how these few words can soften the heart.

Revenge: It is the opposite of forgiveness. To many who seek revenge, they wish to inflict pain, punishment or behave in an action of vengeance in a retaliatory manner. It is hate in behavioral action, so dangerous, and so destructive, for it is a conscious, deliberate act to inflict pain. It is the desire to get even, not necessarily meaning to seek truth and justice. The best antidote is to visualize a court room, where justice prevails and each offender is sentenced accordingly. With justice done there is room now for forgiveness and love is in action. Don't forget to bless yourself and others and go on.

Greed: is excessive desire for material effects, or gluttony. It becomes the substitute for the true desire of the heart, love. If the greed is not diminished it will surely bring self-destruction. The antidote is to pray for the grace to help others. This in time breaks the old selfish habit. With prayer, action and patience the new habit arrives.

Anger: another powerful emotion, for when expressed, the objective is usually seeking to hurt others personally or (their) possessions. The ranges of emotions are rage, fury, wrath, resentment, indignation depending upon situation or circumstance. Some experience this type of anger when faced with a great annoyance, cause of frustration, or antagonized – enraged or troubled. To defeat anger use your free will to repress this destructive emotion. Do the best you can. Go away and pray! Act immediately. Be wise and keep it simple "No anger No regrets." Remember: What you give you give to yourself.

The angry person hurts himself! Bless yourself, go away and pray!

Guilt: is often the result of wrongful action by one that is used to blame another. The element or fact of responsibility not coming to full fruition, neglect, blame, remorse, wrong doing or inadequacy may steer this emotion. The offender may have a seriously troubled or frustrated mind caused by love starvation.

How guilt works

It is important to understand the origin of this highly charged emotion, for if not identified immediately, can manifest in different areas of one's life, thoughts, even behaviors. Example: Case of two brothers -- The older brother, who was adored by the younger one, never missed an opportunity to hurt the younger one over essentially nothing. The older brother's mind somehow picked up a bad vibe that sensed the mother preferred the younger one over him. This type of thinking caused this off-centered belief; therefore his mind became "infected". The younger one reconstructs in his mind the image of unworthiness -- an object for hatred. Ex: He repeatedly was told that is not handy, not mechanically inclined; therefore he is stupid. The hatred is now justified, and becomes cyclical. That's right - repeated many times over and over again in many different settings until it became a man-made behavioral norm. These repetitions had the response in the younger one. He became the perfect fit for his older brother's infected where an unhealthy and extreme codependency developed. The belief that someone had verbal power to make another respond by controlling emotional behavior nurtures self-esteem issues. Result: one not being able to view himself differently as an emotionally independent individual. This fact destroyed the proper perception and therefore much of this person's life.

Now the hurt one state: "Guide to Happiness" enabled me to do a thorough job of spiritual cleansing. This led to a true level of what it means to give and receive the essential love and forgiveness from my older brother. No more emotionally destructive feelings. In fact I am grateful for it the emotionally growing pains through it all. With compassion I got the truth. I got freedom and finally feel at ease!"

Next step of I-identification:

1) Accept the negative feelings -- they happen. This is part of being human and should be reflected upon time to time. Just do your best.
2) Face the sources of the hurtful feelings. They caused lack of acceptance, protection and appreciation which is hard to bear. Facing the source is a step done later through visualization. But first we turn to Science of Reflexology.
3) Since the needed parental love was missing during childhood development, we must sooth the hurtful feelings. "Guide to Happiness "uses Reflexology to serve this purpose. The human body is our neurophysiologic system and its basis for Reflexology has science based principals. It works in Central Nervous System and the integrative center of reflexology called the reticular formation. The reticular formation has a perfect map or an infant style shape, in the brain! (see addendum for reticular formation definition).

Now visualization

Visualize your little body and sweet face living in your heart. Please give, from your heart, all the love and protection a good parent gives to the child. Talk to the child, with your hand on your heart:

"You are the best thing of my life"; "I love you"; "I protect you with all my body, mind and heart." Say until you feel it. If you don't feel it pray to Blessed Mother's Son to help you feel it.

The next step is very important as well

4) Consciously avoid the negative emotions and elevate your feelings, using gratitude.

Gratitude cultivates an elevated state of mind. Ex: Think how many times a day you and I take for granted each breath, $20.000/day. (The free breath is life and it is free. Through gratitude your life blossoms like that of a fresh rose. A rose dries but the essence of our life, like the rose, never dies.) Don't take life, yours or your dear ones, for granted!

5) Practice "active patience". This is step number 4, gratitude for your life with "active patience". "Active patience" is patiently applying the conscious thoughts or wishes repeatedly. This repetition, in time, stimulates the life force from the heart to up-lift the thoughts (see pag.30)

"Active patience" can help you in many diverse ways.

For example, if you have a project, you need a plan. "Active patience" will help avoid omissions, redundancies, glitches and errors of sequence in your plan. (see pag.30)

"Active patience" used consistently, combats passivity and encourages passion for life! When you feel good about your focus mind the whole world is a better place to live.

Never forget:

Words, seemingly innocent, but too often negative, are often prophetic. But prophecy works in the reverse too.
With constantly elevated state of mind and prayer, strive to replace the negative beliefs.
Consistency surely produces results. Try!

During I-identification block, Virginia prayed Rosary, had Reflexology and constantly tries to elevate her state of health with desired announcements. Ex: "I breathe freely and my body is healthy".
Despite everything, Virginia had a brutal anxiety attack while praying The Holy Rosary. Her breathing was so severely affected it led her to feelings of hopelessness.
She was in tears and said: "Mother, please, take me home!"
Instead of receiving "departure" which she had just prayed for, she was gifted with the arrival of normal breathing! From that day on I saw

Virginia progressing. She is now ready to enjoy life since she is no longer tormented by some of the former ailments.

In summary, for the last two years she had visited an array of medical practitioners with unsatisfactory results. The causes of her problems, emotional in nature, were never addressed. But the strong desire to take care of her life brought the fruit from divine intervention. When Virginia had no hope, renewed hope was delivered by the Blessed Mother, the Immaculate Conception from the human heart. Divinity never fails and provides great healing power!

After Virginia had been praying The Holy Rosary and had been following the guide for fourteen months, Easter 2010 came. A friend of Virginia called and told her that while praying to Blessed Mother he learned that Saint Joseph had special feelings for her. On that day, worn out from the Easter dinner preparation, she laid down on her bed.

She said to herself, "It would be so nice to have a father like Saint Joseph!" In that moment, a voice sweet beyond human expression said to her: "I am with you always!"

Then Virginia thought, "From childhood I've known The Father was with us. Lord Jesus Himself named St. Joseph father. *I will do the same.*"

It should be noted that within the joys of meditating "The Holy Rosary" prayer, includes the third block, 2R, removal and simultaneously replacement. Virginia had tremendous help from The Holy Rosary prayer. Therefore she shares with us the joys of meditating upon this prayer. These joys are part of the third block R- remove it, R-replace it.

The first joy - "I discovered humility. God is so humble! He made the human face the image of Himself. Humility is the bed rock of spiritual life, this is certain."

The second joy - take advantage of a short cut. From the words of Teresa of Avila "Why do it the hard way, go to Mary."

Human nature is powerless to heal. In meditation, or while praying The Holy Rosary, the heart is ready for the truth to unfold. In this realization, the truth of heart is the pathway to healing.

Virginia says:

"After much turmoil I realized the great truth: Mary is my mother - She is my real mother!"

Let the "Jewish Mother" heal your hurts, especially when there are deep wounds to the heart. "*We all have a Jewish Mother.*" As expressed by Bob Proctor, International author and master mind teacher.

"The third joy – explained as the warmth of the real maternal love which is unconditional and endless.
When the heart is filled with maternal love, the soul is blissful. This blissful soul empowers the brain, the will and the body. This empowerment is so strong it can deal even with the impossible. This is the true power, the power of parental love. *Parental love,* for me,_is_ first perception of *God, vital for every child.*

The fourth joy - Clarity of thought and 2R-the third block of DI2R

This concentrates on the removal of hurtful images that were within us. This brings clarity of thought! This fourth joy is the third block of DI2R, R-removal of unwanted images so clarity prevails thoughtfully. In this thought process, simultaneous R-replacement interjections begin noticeable healing, designed to be, unique for each person. This sensitive, important concept clearly defines and connects with the top goal of "Guide to Happiness" -- to bring a new blue print. This new blue print reaches good decisions based on love without passing judgment.

About Clarity of Thought

To have clarity of thought, four mini sections are essential:

A) Acceptance of reality – no more lying to the self. No more secrets. Total integrity comes.
The Holy Rosary is a whole and complete prayer and needs to come from a heart both honest and pure. This is the promise of merit beyond measure!

B) Forgiveness of others and of yourself. Now "C" which follows is possible!

C) With wholesome love, I love myself as I am (this is the key to love others as they are).This requires the practice of "active patience "in reality. (in time passion for life arrives, passivity is on the rear burner). See pg. 30.

D) The sign of the cross. It should be self-evident it is the shape of us, the human species. In this shape, the infant in the brain, our life golden-like, lives. Please meditate. Use your sensitivity.

Reminder:

The brain has the mind shape of the human infant, is at one with the body developmentally. Understanding the relationship between body, soul, and mind, we gain insight of ourselves as we come into the balance of good health, wholesomeness and wellness, surrounding us with compassion and forgiveness for ourselves and others. We never forget our goal is to reach love without passing judgment.

Now, we address the four mini sections:

A) Acceptance of reality-no more lying to oneself. No more secrets. Now, the door is open to be moral, honest and filled with integrity.

Virginia disclosed: "My reality is that since childhood I've been unconsciously a participant in thinking as a victim. This primal part of my brain, (within the development of my fetus), where all emotions were created, followed me everywhere. No matter where I went, my unwanted emotions were in my head. This "home" in my head, had my dear ones' attitudes which immersed me in an ocean of criticism, anger and guilt.

But never love. And if nothing else there was indifference, even neglect. For them I was never good enough. I felt empty, humiliated, and therefore sad."

This disclosure brings her naturally to the next indispensable step:

B)   Forgiveness

I said: "Virginia, forgiveness and only forgiveness brings peace of mind. When forgiveness is present there is no room for sadness. The new feelings, at ease, brings in time love. Love heals! Forgiveness is a powerful cleansing process. It is a process of removing the hurt.

However, in order to forgive, we need to be *totally virtuous and filled of integrity.*

Only this level of integrity leads to a "clean glass that holds pure water" (The Blessed Mother). To reach a heightened level of integrity, there must be a strong desire to clean the old house of fear. A fearful soul is insecure so long as the brain doesn't know about love. When the brain knows love the cure is possible. But this love often takes some time, patience and prayer. This is the real antidote for any color, gender, age or race!

Reflect:

In your life's journey, you control the use of the *life's changing word called forgiveness*. In this sense, you are your own savior and the Holy Rosary is your sublime ally!

Assistance for forgiveness

Recall:

When we were young we could not protect ourselves. So we have within us the early emotional hurt we may have experienced where life could be uneasy. Therefore we must allow ourselves to be loved and be kind to ourselves in order to let go of the past. We have to allow ourselves to experience the contrast of being hurt emotionally, and let the essence of us, love, to flow. *The key of letting go of the past is to learn the unknown lesson of loving your mini-body which is in relationship with your thought. Your loving thought is yours mini-body's happiness and his happiness is seen in your successful life.* With your gentleness, which is much powerful than power itself, you bring the infancy stages of your underdeveloped, underused parts of your body into a relationship with the brain now in your heart. Only the heart, the Blessed Mother's home, can embrace the infant, with wisdom, compassion and infinite love. Ask Mother Mary and her Son for help. According to the belief that words have power, in my Holy Rosary prayer the words such as "evil", "sinners", are replaced with the words "fearful thoughts". I then just fold my hands in prayer over the navel with my two thumbs crossed, as a special form of devotion to the Lord.

Forgiveness requires much prayer. In time, the hurt one can turn things around and bless the offender. Oh! Such a freeing feeling, for this is the most powerful sign of healing through the act of forgiveness. Such a blessing to have the love that was lacking and identifying the reason: the needed parental love did not exist. We must sooth the hurtful feelings.

"Guide to Happiness" uses "Heal N.O.W." nothing ordinary works, to calm the mind and sooth the feelings.

Remember -- and refer to the earlier steps and their application. Take that first step. Start by looking deep into your eyes. Then, with a hand on your heart, talk to the image of the one who is very dear to you. "I love you as you are "I love you very much"; "I protect you."

Do this until comfortable. (Virginia used her sons; others one of the parent, others without children used their best spiritual friends, including the spiritual images the Virgin, the Lord…) Image that the Lord is smiling to you: "I am looking in the mirror and I see Me, you look in the mirror and you see Me too".

When your heart is ready, visualize the tiny face of each parent, mother and father, if applicable. Now, from your heart, give all the love and protection to your *mother now a sweet daughter the father an adorable son.*

Say to each of them, yourself included, with your hand on your heart; "You are the best thing of my life", "I love you very much ", "I am always with you and I protect you".

To achieve healing and redemption in the image of "the clean glass that holds the pure water" we must do more about the emotions.

About emotional healing

Virginia found an emotional base in her early years in the lives of her parents. Her grandfather was working long hours; but when at home, he ignored Virginia's father, John.

However his mother was closer to the other children, especially her daughters. She ignored him also.

Because of these parental attitudes, John felt isolated and unloved. Of course he felt rejected. And later all this stressed his physical health to the point of illness. The soul, consisting of the final formation of the child in the brain and the body are partners. As a result, when a child's soul doesn't receive its basic need, love, the body later rebels. If that needy soul receives conscious love, its partner-the body –reacts with joy which leads to good health.

John's body mirrors the missing love. Therefore his physiological disorders include kidney stones and severe lung condition. (Virginia was ignored by him and later developed the same health condition, seriously impaired breathing. Sadly, this was not just a genetic predisposition to disease). *The ignored child mirrors the parent.* "You always hurt the one you love, the one you shouldn't hurt at all."

Virginia's mother

As a young girl the mother was an outstanding student.

After WW2, her widowed mother was struggling to be a good provider for her 7children. At age 10 Virginia's mother had to leave school in order to help her family.

No longer an honor student, she had to work each day with her hands in a factory. This led to bitterness and anger. Her expectations to be an intellectual could not be met; therefore she is unhappy and demanding of others, especially her daughter. Disappointment set in.

Not surprisingly, her health became seriously affected. These emotions, sadness and insecurity, brought her to a point where she became subject to cardiac illness.

Because her anger was so intense her feet were in terrible pain. According to some experts, anger drove her; it was the real basis for painful feet. The calcium was distributed unevenly in the middle of the feet -- crystal like. Lots of pain.

The cartilage-cushion of her joints was compromised and developed chronic arthritis. (unfortunately, probably one of the most painful diseases in these circumstances.)

Now, Virginia, the child of this once joyous, married couple, relates her story:

"My past gave me a sense of insecurity, instability, and rejection. Being single and with major responsibilities and feeling pointed in the wrong direction, I would "beat up" on myself. Unconsciously, I strengthened these destructive elements and my reward was nine physical disorders, none of them trivial.

1. I developed stomach problems - because of fear as the result of following bad decisions. This was somehow reflective of bad attitude and wrong thinking.
2. Lack of joy and love stressed my heart valve; resulting in valve leakage (this condition mirrored the case of my mother).
3. Missing love and protection aggravated insecurity in my life which led to serious cervical and upper body muscular inflammation.
4. The fear of everyday life and its challenges produced extreme shortness of breath. (Never take normal breathing for granted!).

5. Since I lost my father, my life had no sweetness and my insulin levels became imbalanced. In time, this imbalance, I believe, led to acute pancreatitis.
6. Anger and a sort of self-pity, I believe, caused my gallbladder to malfunction. The paradox: my anger was seemingly justified. Yet, it aggravated my medical condition.

Here is a basic rule. *Anger begets more anger.* The outcome is the body suffers and gets sick. In order to treat the condition my job is the need to know the cause and administer treatment. I know love is missing. The solution is to help the individual identify what it is, and then show how to fill the void – the missing love. My advice: love and protect the purity of your baby in the *brain, pray Holy Rosary, practice active patience.* Of course have "Hidden Energy-*ReflexOlogy* for body, mind and heart. This _care and love heals_. Now back to Virginia.

7. Humiliation over time caused chemical imbalance.
   Iodine, zinc, potassium deficiency led to Thyroid disorder which included severe swelling of the throat and overweight (the emotional eating).
8. Since I could not speak to protect myself, when young, I believe over time I developed gum disease.
9. To complete the ugly package clinging to the past made me a candidate for colonic problems."

Virginia, obviously impressed asked, "How can thoughts be so powerful and often truly destructive?"

I said, "Though is life and life is feeling with emotion. Because the old hurtful emotions originating from your "childlike status in your brain" are still with you, you carry them. You will always carry them in the 'coded map' where the infant shape is located – your memory. And the 'body' formation one develops within the brain reacts, reflects, and forms attractions to stimuli.

Remember: emotional disorder can involve the psychological, the physical, the financial and throughout all your relationships. Now you understand what "illness" means in context of your life. Contextually, you can understand *why* there was emotional hurt and pain, *its origin,* and manifestations as end *result.* These *damaged emotions operate as broken or irrational thoughts* (skewed), which become actualized. Outcome: a sense of damaged perception and skewed thoughts. These damaged emotions, parallel or coupled with formed thoughts; need to be Detected, Identified and Removed-Replaced. (DI2R)

We want to stop them from becoming core in our belief. The belief usually generates a *repetitive message or announcement send through the brain communicating our unwanted reality – contextually, created irrational, disordered thinking.*

In this understanding, we acknowledge that these damaged emotions behind our old thoughts come from a place where love was mostly neglected or hurt.

Active patience is a habit of thought. This active patience preserves order in the very life of the body. Through the wisdom of "Guide to Happiness" protection is assured and you learn *how to gain and maintain the greatest happiness principles.*

Now comes the key point: Pay attention to the signals of your body, and dig for the emotional causes.

Example:

John's anger makes his blood pressure high. John is now on-notice to control his anger. Perhaps he needs to use DI2R where he can begin with repetitive health announcements such as, "My life is joyful and my mind and body is healthy. I love myself."

As the mind and emotions need help, the body needs help as well. Some of this help involves physical release.

What does 'physical release' mean? When do I recommend physical release? Answer: "Confront in the mind's eye, (the area in the brain where emotions are stored), *all the hurtful actions, the words, and faces.* The tension and grief created by old emotions should come out through a physical release. This release helps dissolve the old frustration, blame and anger. And in time, makes room for compassion and empathy.

In the recall of old emotions, many possibilities exist.

For a pragmatic person, as your author, some extreme measures were fruitful: crying, rage, beating the pillows, kickboxing, all of which can relive the pain. Another modest example, which I tried, was care taker for animals, plants and birds. Seeking *justice,* which *heals,* you should reflect upon those who have hurt you. Perhaps the following metaphor will help. Bring them to your court room, where you are the *fair judge* and justice is fairly served.

Again you may visualize the baby from the brain -having your face looking at you, the parent, and then at those who have hurt you so much. Maybe a sentence can then be handed down with an equitable punishment.

Now, to you – Virginia, as a whole person, child and judge, can conceptualize and understand that *you didn't know how to protect the purity of your own mini-body.* That perhaps the *ones who hurt you are like you,* - they didn't know how to protect either. If they had known, they would have protected the purity of their innocence from the brain, the infants, and they would protect you too. Now, *the purity of your mini-body (mind, soul) is free from those who were unhealed children* (abusive). In other words, your soul is safe and secure with you, the parent, who fills the void with encouragements and loving thoughts. Your love with Christ passion from your thoughts gives back to you what you give. Life.
Never, ever criticize yourself or others!

Besides Reflexology, Virginia keeps the Holy Rosary close to her heart. It is her spiritual umbilical cord (lifeline) uniting her to her divine parents.

In this important period of challenge she has conversation with like-minded people. She practices selectivity with the media, reads and studies worthwhile material.

The penultimate step of "Guide to Happiness" gives the formula for changing the thought pattern of the mind in order to heal the damaged emotion. In time this formula will change reality.

The formula has three critical steps. We start with most common complaint "not being good enough". We've been told so often we are not good enough we believe it and make it reality. To change this reality we must dispel this belief.

Step 1-Pray to Release the Affliction and Its Cause

This requires the nurturing relationship and kindness of a good parent to the self (remember the baby).

Virginia, when you fail to treat yourself with kindness, you think you resist an unwanted, but familiar feeling - being hurt. Since you *mistrust the kindness, you go* with the familiar cognitive behavior of *"what you know and you don't want".* This is a cyclical behavior that needs to be broken through a change in thought pattern. Otherwise, there is behavior regression. The result is an appearance of *self-inflicted pain.* This unwanted feeling easily becomes your *personal truth,* your belief. For instance, in the spiritual, when you have an enemy he is omnipresent. When you fail to pray, your enemy is with you everywhere. Since he is your truth at that moment in time, he confirms the reality of your belief. But when you have compassion for your enemy, because compassion is your belief, you help yourself. You are now liberated from the unwanted enemy, unwanted belief and unwanted reality. Therefore, remember this: "How many times do we have to forgive?" Compassion for an unhealed child requires the same number, 70 times multiplied by 7. For your soul – well, you decide.

Step I) - Prayer is Required for Unwanted Belief

"I pray for those who viewed me as not good enough. I pray to release this feeling of inadequacy and with it any fear of not being good enough".

With your hand on your heart, using your best smile, visualize your infant. Change your thinking and reflect upon what your mind is saying. It tells you that smiling people are the most beautiful. And you want your child to see you beautiful. *You want your spirit and soul healed.*

Step II) -Strengthen the Emotion. Build New Beliefs: "I am a whole entire person." "I learned compassion for me and forgiveness for those who have hurt me." "I am adequate to meet every challenge." "I am happy."

Step III)-Virginia, with your hand on your heart you may address what some call ultimate healing:

"I pray for all people that touched my life, my parents and others, as well for me to live without judgment. Live life with love and com-passion."

I am a strong believer in this philosophy, and I view this as a cause and effect – or a priori (the greatest happiness principle). This ultimate goal requires the greatest effort in prayer but the reward exceeds your effort.

Note: Initially this may seem like lip service but ask God, Blessed Mother's Son, to make it real.

These three forms of release require only 3min, 3 times /day.

Virginia addresses her problem:

"I lacked joy and love"

This stressed Virginia to a point of a leaking heart valve. For this leaking valve she does these steps 3min, 3 times/, day.

I) Virginia prays to release the affliction and its cause

"I pray to Blessed Mother's Son to release the affliction of a leaking heart valve and with it the cause, the fear of being guilty and not loved."

Note:

The mind (includes the soul) and the heart is one. When the mind fails to transmits love, the heart may have a leaking valve.

Train and pray for your mind to be non-judgmental; this can be the way to a healthy and a loving heart as well. Take notice of Virginia's steps:

II) Strengthen the emotion she has gained from the first step

"My heart beats at once with Mother Mary's. I have now her personal guaranty that I am safe and loved".

III) Achieve the ultimate healing

"I pray for all people that touched my life and for me to live without judgment and therefore with love and passion for life". This requires the greatest effort in prayer but give gratitude to you for making the effort.

Virginia's Shoulder Pain Addressed

This pain often can be traced to poor emotional support. Over stimulated and exhausted nerves often lead to shoulder pain (remember: exhausted nerves pinch the shoulder much as bad news automatically brings "a punch in the gut".

I) Pray to release the affliction

"I pray to release the affliction of shoulder pain and with it the fear of lacking support".

II) Strengthen the gained emotion

"Blessed Mother's Son is always with me; therefore, I have healthy shoulders." Meditation and visualization is important.

III) Achieve the ultimate healing

"I pray for all people that touched my life and for me to live without judgment and therefore with passion for life."

Shortness of breath

The repression of intuition intensified the tension of everyday life which gave me severe shortness of breath.

I) Pray to release the affliction of shortness of breath.

"I pray to release the affliction of shortness of breath and with it the fear of endless repression of the intuitive power."

II) Strengthen the emotion

"Through the Blessed Mother's Son the real breath of life arrived. I breathe freely. Thank you! I am so grateful!"

III) Achieve the ultimate healing

"I pray for all people that touch my life and for me to live without judgment and therefore with passion for life".

Virginia continues:

"I felt rejected. Much anger and frustration caused life to lose its sweetness. My body reacted with an inflamed pancreas."

As before we use 3 steps

I) Pray to release

"I pray to release the affliction of inflamed pancreas and with it the anger and frustration."

II) Strengthen the emotion

"Through Blessed Mother the real life arrived. My life is sweet again."

III) Achieve the ultimate healing

"I pray for all people that touched my life and for me to live without judgment and therefore with love and passion for life."

Virginia addresses the gallbladder

With mixed sadness and anger I would say, "Why me?" So, the gallbladder responded accordingly.

Remember: The entire physical body responds to uncontrolled anger and the sadness which follow. This can create an emotional and physical mess within you, or you can recognize in a wholesome way the changes in your thought pattern required for a healing, appreciate the signal and look for causation with end result in undergoing treatment.

As before we follow 3steps:

I) Pray to release the affliction

"I pray to release the affliction of an imbalanced gallbladder; and along with it, the sadness and anger."

II) Strengthen the gained emotion

"Blessed Mother gave me the best thing of her life, a Divine Son and herself a Virgin am so much honored ,balanced and I am very happy!"

III) Achieve the ultimate healing

"I pray for all people that touched my life and for me to live without judgment; and therefore, I pray to live with love and passion for life."

Virginia continues:

"Since I felt so insignificant and humiliated the thyroid suffers imbalance.

I) Pray to release the affliction

"I pray to release the affliction of thyroid imbalance; and along with it, the fear of being insignificant and humiliated."

II) Strengthen the gained emotion

"Through Blessed Mother and her Son the fear of being insignificant is gone along with the feeling of being humiliated. I am worthy. I am so grateful! Thank you!"

III) Achieve the ultimate healing

"I pray for all people that touched my life and for me to live without judgment. I, therefore, live with love and passion for life."

Virginia goes on:

"My resentment boiled over into desire to take revenge. Because my faculty to speak for myself failed, my gums are chronically affected. I did the required 3 steps, 3min, 3 times/day".

I) Pray to release the affliction.

"I pray to release the affliction of gum disease, and with it, the fear of endless repression of not speaking for myself."

II) Strengthen the gained emotion

"Through Blessed Mother's Son the truth of life arrived. I speak my truth freely."

III) Achieve the ultimate healing

"I pray for all people that touched my life and for me to live without judgment; and therefore, live with Christ love and com-passion for *life*."

Finally Virginia says:

"Clinging to the past seemed to be an emotional blockage which leads to colonic problem."

I did the requirements, 3min, and 3times/day.

I) I pray to release

"I pray to release the affliction of blockages and with it all the hurtful experiences which are toxins from the past."

II) Virginia strengthens the gained emotion

"I clean my emotional map with the powerful cleansers, compassion, forgiveness and love for me, for them, for life. When this is done the emotional map (infant shape) has abundance of fresh air. Right amount of oxygen results in a body which has a healthy digestive system".

III) Achieving ultimate healing

"I pray for all people that touched my life and for me to live without judgment; and therefore, live with love and passion for life."

Virginia's mother's resentment of authority that may have led to arthritic pain can use the same three steps.

I) She can pray to release the affliction

"I pray to release the affliction of arthritic pain and with it the fear of financial instability, life's safeness."

II) The mother of Virginia can strengthen the gained emotion

"Through Blessed Mother's Son who took away the real life's safeness, worked through me and people who love me. The provision of financial stability arrived. I live pain free."

III) Achieving the ultimate healing

"I pray for all people that touched my life, my family and myself to live within love and forgiveness and never be punished on my account."

Other cases

Mr. M. and his rashes (skin problem).

Each new born baby wishes to be the center of parental attention and love.

Lack of parental love, seriously damaged the emotions of Mr. M were identified. This emotional upset, so extensive, went into overtime and caused serious skin rashes.

Mr. M's case demonstrates the need for this rule.

He did the required steps 3 min, 3 times/day

I) He prayed to release the affliction

"I pray to release the affliction of rashes. Together with prayer, I use the exercises of self-help until the proper self-love arrives. This provides compassion and love for me - the child now in my heart."

II) He strengthens the gained emotion

"Through prayer to Blessed Mother I receive special maternal warmth." With my hand on my heart I say aloud: "I love myself." "I am loved and I have healthy skin".

III) Achieving ultimate healing

"I pray for all people that touched my life, my family and myself to live within love and unconditional forgiveness".

Mr.M said: "Now, I believe every *child comes from his parents' spiritual mind, the body and heart and he lives with them in the same triune home, the autonomic nervous system and heart.*"

Another case is Mrs. J and her obesity problem.

I said, "Poor self-esteem (sense of unworthiness) often leads to obesity. This pattern of low self-esteem which includes missing love and compassion for the child needs to be conquered (otherwise fear of not being good enough and overeating continues). This because the child is your life and he loves your body because it is the best thing of his life. Therefore he expects unconditional love. If not the child will fill the void with food, alcohol, cigarette, drugs, sex or similar friends. These are the tools to use.

I) Please pray to release the affliction

I pray to Mother Mary to release the affliction of obesity and with it the fear of feeling unworthy, guilty and unwanted. We can see how the effect always asks us to work with the cause.

II) Strengthen the emotions:

I change my eating behavior and I smile (smiling people burns calories). Therefore my image becomes, in time, the desired one. "My body is slender, worm and athletic. Hard work on treadmill or dancing teaches me to push my physical limits. I appreciate what my body can do."

III) Achieving the ultimate healing

"I pray for all people that touched my life, my family and those who need a prayer to live within Christ's love and com-passion."

Mrs.'S. She is underweight

A person who misses the wholesome love tends to be underweight.

I) Pray to release the affliction

"I pray to Blessed Mother's Son to release the fear of emptiness and being unloved. I have the desired weight."

II) She strengthens the gained emotion

"I retain the important rewards inside of me, the courage and clarity", "I am loved and I am fit".

III) Achieving the ultimate healing

"I pray for all people that touched my life, my family and myself to live with faith, forgiveness, love and gentleness."

Now back to Virginia

The last step of the DI2R of the "Guide to Happiness" is the most important. I name it Ultimate Imagery. This exercise is designed to arouse in you the purity of love. This beautiful love flows from the child in the brain as it must.

In this step you image the person's eyes that have hurt you. Looking deeply into this person's eyes, you look actually into yourself, because we are the mirror of each other. Doing this exercise is so essential because if you mistakenly hurt the offender, you can no longer see yourself. And <u>*you must be able to see yourself!*</u>

We can do this exercise through visualization or looking in to the eyes of another.

The exercise has two parts. Part one is from the hurt one: "I am life. I came from the heart in one body, as yours, to bring joy and happiness. Through you, I find the truth. You have been my best teacher. I learned human life's essential lessons of love and unconditional forgiveness. Thank you! I forgive you, love you and I set you free."

The second part is from the offender, "I loved you the best way I could according to my own awareness, humanism and limitations. I love you and I set you free".

Virginia, I believe every child comes from his parents' mind where the spiritual intelligence and heart lives; there lies unconditional love. The parents' mind, the spiritual intelligence and unconditional love, lives in the third party within the child in his mind, the spiritual intelligence and heart.

In your case, Virginia, the foot print, your father was not present; and this of course served to make your mother unhappy.

Therefore you were in an environment where spiritual intelligence and unconditional love was missing. This environment was an uncomfortable place, unfortunately your old mind, which had the spiritual intelligence but had not the unconditional love. Therefore you were looking everywhere for the higher ground or better place and your life for a while was chaotic.

Virginia says quite softly, *"My life is now restored. I now have the blissful spirit of life and the wisdom of self-worth."*

We are finished with this last phase of "Guide to Happiness." It has been hard to do and it is hard to write about, but worth every minute.

Appreciations

"Dear Deniza D., when I came to" "Heal N.O.W.".-<u>nothing</u> <u>ordinary</u> <u>works,</u> I had medical problems which were unresolved. Through your treatments I received great results. But some of them remained. To solve the cause of these problems I came to use "Guide to Happiness". In use of "Guide to Happiness" the fruits of my efforts were met with much power and success.

Since I was enlightened with the sure knowledge of the child in my brain, I could do the steps of wholesome self –love needed to reach forgiveness. I now have peace of mind as well as a sense of joy. Much time and much effort but with such sweet results.

Thank you again! Ms. Ida W. Judge

Mr. Jude and Vertigo

"I was the victim of a vicious vertigo attack. It was so severe it seemed my head would split in order to release its contents. And terrible nausea was with it. Unable to drive I reached my reflexologist who provided prompt treatment. In one session she restored my health to normalcy. There has been no relapse. Her results were so remarkable, so astounding!

I am so grateful!

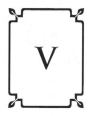

Testimonials

Virginia's testimonial

This concept, the purity of an infant in the brain, helped me to discover reciprocal love, compassion and protection. This very deep love makes in time the strongest base for a healthy and happy life. Therefore it becomes a mission to deliver to those who unfortunately, as myself, had the *unconscious need for self - destruction.*

I highly recommend "Guide to Happiness-Boot Camp for 21st Century" to those who are really convinced that *right now* health and happiness is attainable. And if you are not convinced read it until you are convinced.

Time is precious!

With "Guide to Happiness" I guaranty you will not lose anything, not even time.

I the author must mention that now Virginia has a husband who said: "Love is Jesus who lives in people's heart". Time has served them well. Be in love with your dear one in your own heart it projects the very theme of this book.

Don's testimonial

Some months ago I met my reflexologist, Deniza D. She was able to provide great relief for the physical symptoms and soon she placed me into re- writing desk of "Guide to Happiness".

During this time, 48 month, I was able to clean my mental house much more than I did without "Guide to Happiness" in 30 years, (I started when I was 50 years old!).

The author's belief about the child in the brain

After many years I discovered the astounding truth that each person has an infant in the brain. This amazing truth is scientific fact. But it is little known. Reference: Dr.Manzanares Reflexologic Method student work book.

I believe that the body in the brain is the man consciousness that sees in each human heart God.

Believe me or not, completing this "Guide" will bring to your life health, abundance, wisdom and peace.

This is a paradox that in my life's journey the most painful chapters are the most useful.

I know that everything is God and I always have had the free will. Therefore I believe I chose all my experiences and nobody has to pay in my account. It is the opposite, I am grateful to them all.

VII

How I got the basis for "Guide to Happiness"

My sources for "Guide to Happiness" include my decision to help children, my sons and Law School. In Law School I learned the concept of "baby's cortex has a map which contains certain indicators. These indicators, can be read by specialists who can make the judgments of the potential of each baby". Law School is a priceless education. It helps to solidify, organize and discipline the integrity of the brain! But with this perception the living can be hard!

Also this education prepared my brain to realize that I am surrounded with much greater, loving and intelligent mind of course superior to my own, Lord Jesus. The next contributor is the Manzanares instructor, Charlotte Irwin. She taught me to become a certified reflexologist of this scientist.

The next major contributor is Dr. Manzanares, himself. I attended to his 16 hours presentation of the "Principles of Reflexology", DR. Manzanares Method, Los Angeles, CA.

A great source is Dr. Tom Sannar classes (SOM).He teaches spiritual mind's treatment and conscious control of the free-will aimed at positive images in order to exclude unwanted imagery.

The ultimate source is my insatiable curiosity and grace for God, Jesus and Mary. This loving faith brought me to prayer, fasting and meditation to include pleading for answers (with many tears).

I express all my appreciation to my essential sources which includes of course my grandmothers, both named Mary, my parents, my sons and my friends of all persuasions.

Also special thanks to my dear Muslim Turkish mentor; Ali (Omer). His influence for four years is *the key* for my spiritual growth!

I make a special mention of the Magheti Romanian family. They helped me, a single, confused but dedicated mother, to come to USA. This decision led to great results. I am the parent and the person I wanted to be, not any more single or confused. The best of all, conflict and frustration is replaced with humor. Lord Jesus has humor! This makes me *a winner!*

My gratitude to my best friend, Mr. Don, who assisted at the rewriting desk. He is what, as a child saw in my parents, the goodness of God. Because of his integrity, intelligence and purity of heart he is what my infant really needed, the Saintly father's figure, and the male soul of this program.

I am grateful beyond measure to the Lord. He has not only given Himself to me but He has given the best thing of His life, the Blessed Mother from the beginning in my heart. The Queen of Hope loves with No exception all of us and she is the sure way to her Divine Son who makes with her children one Virgin heart where they are safe and loved. Such bliss.

In order to achieve this bliss *I had to learn to be responsible for the success of my own life*. My early life involved so much hurt that even at tender age at 9 I formed the decision to help children to find a loving family. In order to help others it seemed necessary to have that hurt and to do "Guide to Happiness". Since my own reality has now evolved I am ready to help others. Note: The unseen becomes seen only through our faith, God.

With this Guide, I have helped myself and children to find a new-mind blue print. This blue print is to love our parents as we love ourselves because we are *one body* with them. The best images to love in our parents is God, the Virgin Mother and The Lord. This love will be in our body and family life from inside will be restored and reality. This new family brings the right partners in our life and our children are loved. Because of it our children will make good decisions and they and their children will love and will be loved.

Deniza is your author's name. It is similar to a son's name, Deniz. Deniz means ocean (ocean -of love- from where we are all born to live abundantly)

Recommendation:

This Guide requires five major things:

1) Your decision to save your life,
2) The willingness to pray "The Holy Rosary" which restores your spiritual mind,
3) Relax your brain with "Heal N.O.W.-nothing ordinary works",
4) Essential enlightened self –love. The thought with love promotes serotonin. No more anxiety or depression. Life!
5) A com-passionate family member, friend or therapist.

For my customized prayer and service email me: guide2happiness@ gmail.com

We wish to assist parents in fulfilling their obligation to educate themselves and their children in "Why Worry-Go to Mary", W.G.T.M. International Organization. This includes the practice of Faith: Love and Unconditional Forgiveness. *Faith is* the best education since *Mary's honor and Jesus's glory* exist in *one's mind and heart.*

James 1:12 "Religion that God our Father accepts as pure and faultless is this: *To look after orphans and widows in their distress and to keep oneself from being polluted by the world*".

PS. Profits from this program will be used for this segment of people through through " Heal N.O.W." International Organization

Change Ordinary Beliefs to Extraordinary Tradition and Culture of the Virgins

VIII

Addendum

From Wikipedia

"The reticular formation is a region in the brain stream. It is the "sentinel" of the Reticular Active System and selects the stimuli. RAS is the brain's command and control system, centered with consciousness, in the thalamus, which sends and receives signals to and all parts of the brain and body. But, the Reticular Formation not only selects important stimuli, it removes **_99+% from our very perception._**

"***We are living in a post-hypnotic trance, induced in early infancy.***" ***R.D.Lang*** (some cases included in the womb)

The RF/RAS generates responses or response- impulses to fulfill our creative acts of Will, Commitment and Imagination. RAS/RF works continuously to bring us Serenity, Peace and takes responsibility for the Love/Belief System.

Nothing need change but our hearts. There need to be the Virgins of us! This is how we begin to live in an open brain and a sparkling world.

In preparing my protocol, beside Reflexology, I used the Vertebral Subluxation and Nerve Chart, the Vertebral Emotional Chart, the 32 Chakras and the Spine Chart, Acupressure Foot Chart, the tuning forks, crystals, oils and prayer.

P.S. When I treat I fast. By fasting I know that my client and I share the same belief. He believes that he can be helped and I believe I can do it. My Faith not only believes is something to happen, it has already happened. Only the mind needs to be relaxed. This is the only "mountain" to the person's awesomeness.

Note: Digestive System plays an important role in our health. Stress failed my ileocecal valves and my whole body suffered.

About diet I tell to my clients about the 6th commandment" though shall not kill" is expended to protect not only humans but the animals as well. They might try fortified diet of seed, greens, vegetable and fruits with eggs and dairy products. But who are concern about being unable to meet healthy protein requirements here are the animals flesh accepted by most Rabbi's today. The Lord Himself was a Rabbi. This includes cattle, sheep, goats, deer, bison, chicken, geese, ducks and turkey.

Sometimes I tell to my clients this recommendation:" No virus lives in this Oregano oil."(This is much more impressive than the prescription or words we often get).

Some examples of my 3'/3 times /day affirmations:

I love my occupation. It is my passion and my life purpose.

I am connected with clients whom I can best serve.

My clients are happy to pay good money for themselves getting treatment from me.

I live rich, active and longer serving and teaching people to live the same.

My family, neighbors and friends are my loving support. We are all in one home. Life is good!

In the healing journey Louise Hay, the author of "You Can Heal Your Life" found great value in Reflexology as she treated her own case of cancer. Her book is my inspiration and assisted me in my healing journey. Thank you very much!

Lawrence Wilson, MD, the author of "Nutritional Balancing and Hair Mineral Analysis a New Science of Energy "recommends Reflexology for the structural problems which can affect one's thinking and actions.

And can help correct the brain architecture.